W9-AAL-069

Barnard Environmental Magnet School
170 Derby Avenue
New Haven, CT 06511

What is a
Living Thing?

A Bobbie Kalman Book

 Crabtree Publishing Company

www.crabtreebooks.com

The Science of Living Things Series

A Bobbie Kalman Book

To Debbie Wenger
for keeping my life in order

Author and Editor-in-Chief
Bobbie Kalman

Managing editor
Lynda Hale

Editors
April Fast
Heather Levigne
Kate Calder

Computer design
Lynda Hale

Production coordinator
Hannelore Sotzek

Special thanks to
Nicole Hill; Craig Eady; Victorian Eady; Mark Jones;
Teva Wood; Megan Peters; Jody and Justin Pepe;
Danielle Kessel; and Olivia, Adrien, and Marianne Baude

Photographs
Andre Baude: page 21 (both)
Russell C. Hansen: page 24 (bottom)
Christl Hill: page 30
Bobbie Kalman: pages 15 (inset), 17
Dwight R. Kuhn: page 19 (top)
James H. Robinson: page 29 (top)
Sylvia Stevens: page 19 (bottom)
Other photographs by Digital Stock and Digital Vision

Illustrations
Barbara Bedell: pages 6, 8 (cells and leaves), 9, 10, 11,
    13, 14, 18-19, 20-21, 23, 25 (bottom), 26, 28, 29
Antoinette "Cookie" Bortolon: pages 8 (boy), 25 (top)
Jeanette McNaughton-Julich: page 17
Bonna Rouse: pages 4-5

Crabtree Publishing Company

www.crabtreebooks.com   1-800-387-7650

Cataloging in Publication Data
Kalman, Bobbie
    What is a living thing?
(The science of living things)
Includes index.
ISBN 0-86505-879-2 (library bound) ISBN 0-86505-891-1 (pbk.)
This book introduces living things, including people, other animals, and plants, and
covers such topics as breathing, feeding, energy, growth, movement, and reproduction.
1. Biology—Juvenile literature. [1. Life (Biology) 2. Biology.] I. Title. II. Series: Kalman,
Bobbie. Science of living things.
QH309.2.K25 1999   j570   LC 98-30913
                                                                                CIP

**Published in
the United States**
PMB 16A
350 Fifth Ave.
Suite 3308
New York, NY
10118

**Published
in Canada**
616 Welland Ave.
St. Catharines, Ontario
L2M 5V6

**Published in the
United Kingdom**
White Cross Mills
High Town, Lancaster
LA1 4XS

**Published
in Australia**
386 Mt. Alexander Rd.
Ascot Vale (Melbourne)
VIC 3032

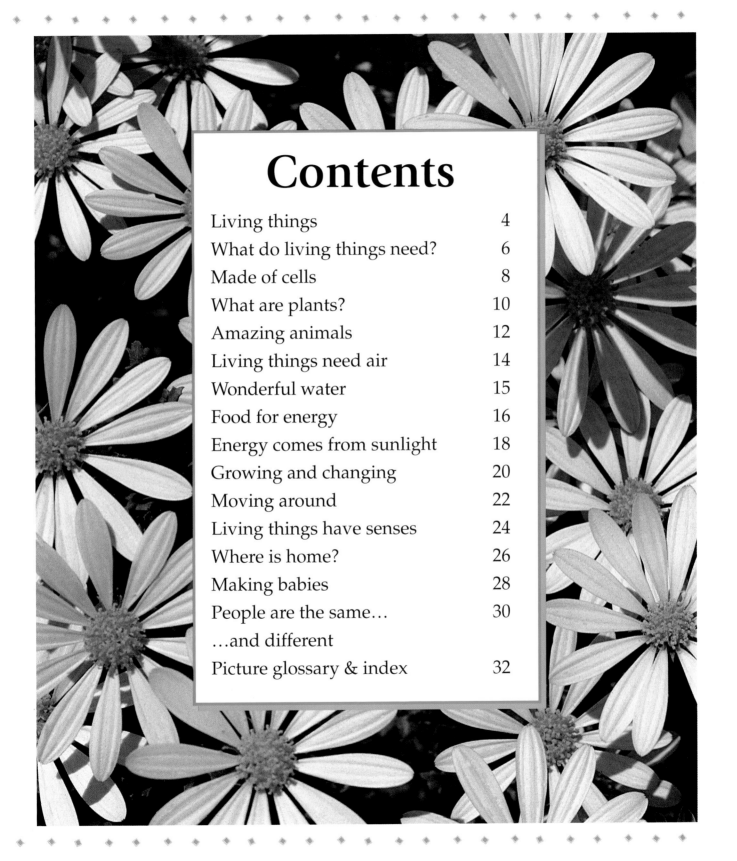

Contents

Living things

Look at the pictures on these pages. Some of the things are living, and some are not. How can you tell if something is a living thing?

Does a chair breathe air?

Does a table eat food?

Does a teddy bear drink water?

Do toys need sunlight?

Do books grow?

Do computers have babies?

The answer to all these questions is no. These things are not living. Name all the living things in this picture.

Answers:
trees, flowers,
2 rabbits, 2 fish
5 plants in pots,
6 people,
1 cat, 1 dog

What do living things need?

Living things need air, food, and water. Most living things need sunlight. They also need places to live. Plants and animals need all these things to stay alive.

You are a living thing, too. You
need air, water, food, and sunshine.
Living things need other living
things. You need plants and
animals. You need other people.

Made of cells

Every living thing is made of **cells**. A cell is so tiny that you cannot see it with just your eyes. You need a microscope to see it.

Most of the living things on Earth have only one cell. Other living things are made up of many kinds of cells. Each kind of cell has a special job to do.

These green cells are plant cells.

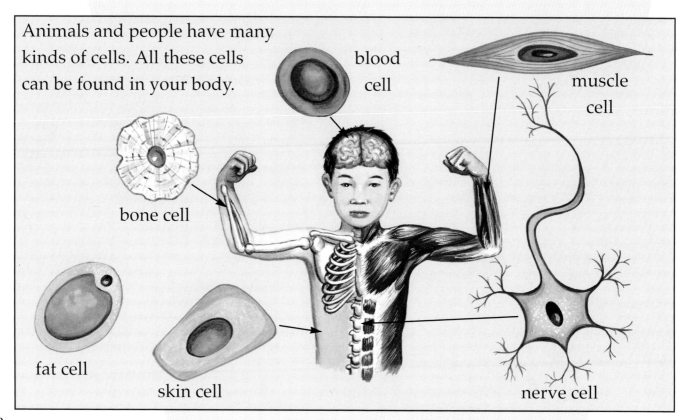

Animals and people have many kinds of cells. All these cells can be found in your body.

blood cell

muscle cell

bone cell

fat cell

skin cell

nerve cell

There are five kinds of living things. Each box on this page shows a different kind.

1. Some tiny living things such as **bacteria** are made of one simple cell. Bacteria that can make you sick are called **germs**.

2. Amoebae are also tiny living things that have just one cell. Unlike bacteria, amoebae have center parts called **nuclei**.

3. Mushrooms and toadstools are not plants. They are living things called **fungi**.

4. Trees, bushes, flowers, and weeds are plants.

5. Birds, insects, snakes, and fish are animals. People also belong to this group of living things. Name some other animals that you know.

What are plants?

Plants are living things. They are the only living things that can make food from light, air, and water. Most plants have roots, leaves, and stems.

Plants can live in soil, sand, and water. They can even grow on rocks.

Plants give off a gas that people and animals need to breathe. This gas is **oxygen**. Plants also help make the air cleaner to breathe. They take in a gas called **carbon dioxide**. Too much carbon dioxide is harmful to people and animals.

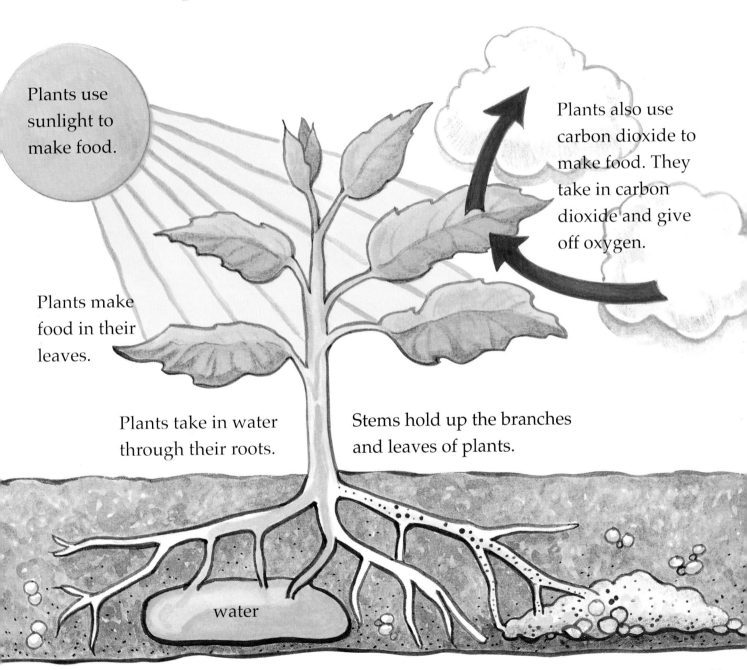

Plants use sunlight to make food.

Plants also use carbon dioxide to make food. They take in carbon dioxide and give off oxygen.

Plants make food in their leaves.

Plants take in water through their roots.

Stems hold up the branches and leaves of plants.

water

Amazing animals

Animals can be as small as fleas or as large as elephants. There are many kinds of animals. Birds, bats, insects, fish, and frogs are animals.

Animals need plants and other animals. They need **habitats**, or places to live. Animals live in water and on land. They live in hot and cold places.

Animals without a backbone are called **invertebrates**. Invertebrates come in different shapes.

Squids have tentacles and heads with eyes.

The bodies of jellyfish are made up of stomachs and **tentacles**.

Sponges suck in food through holes.

Sea stars have five arms.

Insects are the only invertebrates that can fly.

Crabs have six legs and claws.

Worms have long, thin bodies.

Animals that have backbones are called **vertebrates**. The animals in this box are vertebrates.

Bears and mice are **mammals**. Female mammals make milk to feed their young.

Most fish live only in water.

Frogs are **amphibians**. They live on land and in water.

Snakes and other **reptiles** have scaly skin.

All birds have beaks and feathers.

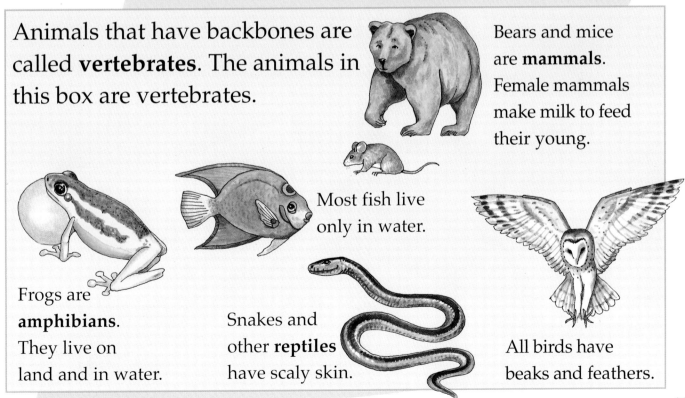

Living things need air

Earth is the only planet in our solar system that has air. Air covers Earth like a blanket. It helps protect living things from the sun's burning rays.

Earth is the only planet that we know of that has living things. Living things need the oxygen and carbon dioxide in air to stay alive.

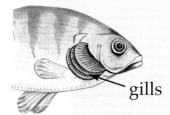

gills

People and many other animals breathe air using **lungs**.

Fish live in water. They take in oxygen through their gills.

This mud puppy lives in water and breathes through gills around its neck. It also takes in oxygen through its skin.

spiracles

Insects breathe through **spiracles** along both sides of their body.

Plants take in carbon dioxide through holes called **stomata** on the under-sides of their leaves.

gills

Wonderful water

All living things need water to stay alive. Your body needs water to carry oxygen and food to all its cells. To help stay healthy, you need to drink at least eight glasses of water every day. Don't wait until you are thirsty!

Food   for energy

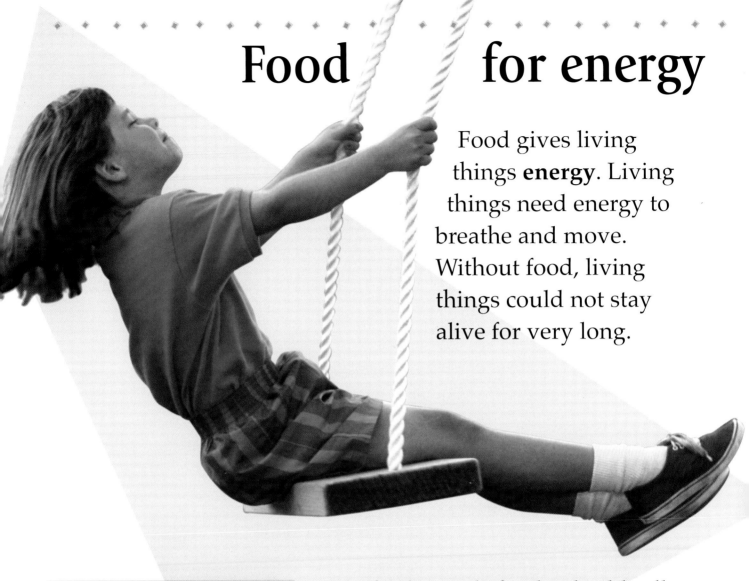

Food gives living things **energy**. Living things need energy to breathe and move. Without food, living things could not stay alive for very long.

Your body needs food to build cells so you can grow. Milk, meats, breads, fruits, and vegetables are some of the foods that help keep you healthy. These foods come from other living things. Fruits, vegetables, and breads come from plants. Meats, eggs, and some kinds of milk come from animals.

"Hooray for fruit!
Apples and pears
are a healthy snack!"

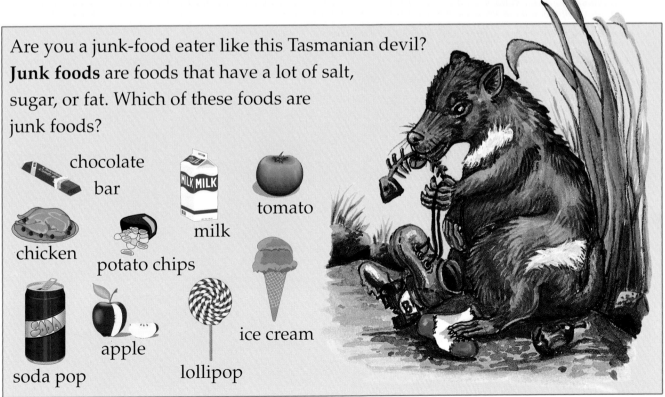

Are you a junk-food eater like this Tasmanian devil?
Junk foods are foods that have a lot of salt,
sugar, or fat. Which of these foods are
junk foods?

chocolate bar

milk

tomato

chicken

potato chips

ice cream

soda pop

apple

lollipop

Energy comes from sunlight

The cabbage uses the sun's energy to grow.

The rabbit gets the sun's energy from eating the cabbage.

The wolf gets the sun's energy from eating the rabbit.

You get energy from the foods you eat. The energy in food comes from sunlight. The sun's energy is passed along from living thing to living thing in a **food chain**.

Plants use the energy in sunlight to make food. Plants make their own food, but animals cannot. Animals need to eat plants or other animals.

Some animals get the sun's energy when they eat plants. Others get the sun's energy when they eat animals that have eaten plants.

The cabbage, rabbit, and wolf form one food chain. The berries, mouse, and owl on the next page form another food chain.

The berries in this picture are part of a plant. They are full of the sun's energy. When the mouse eats the berries, it is getting the energy of the sun.

When the owl eats the mouse, it will get the energy of the sun, too. The sun's energy is in the berries, and the berries are inside the mouse. Very soon, the mouse will be inside the owl!

Growing and changing

Trees grow taller and wider.

Plants and animals grow bigger as they get older. They change in other ways, too. The leaves of many trees change colors in autumn and drop off the branches. Birds lose their feathers and grow new ones. Some living things change when their habitats change. These kinds of changes can take thousands or millions of years!

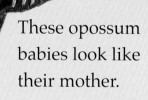

These opossum babies look like their mother.

Some living things look like their parents when they are born. Other living things go through big changes as they grow. These changes are called **metamorphosis**. The pictures along the bottom of these pages show the metamorphosis of a ladybug beetle.

eggs

larva

pupa

When children grow, their bodies change in many ways. Their legs and arms grow longer, and their hands and feet grow bigger.

Their hair grows too, and often the color changes. Children lose their baby teeth when they are five or six years old. Permanent teeth grow in their place.

The picture above was taken ten years after the one on the left. Name all the ways each child in these pictures has grown and changed. How have you changed since you were a baby?

new adult

adult

Moving around

Some living things are able to move, and others stay in the same place. Plants cannot change where they live, but they can move! Daisies close their petals at night. Sunflowers turn their heads to face the sun as it moves across the sky during the day.

These springboks can run quickly and take big leaps with their long, strong legs.

The baby Komodo dragon can climb trees.

Animals move to get food, find a mate, or escape from their enemies. They move in many different ways. Dogs run, frogs hop, fleas jump, snakes slither, fish swim, and most birds fly.

People can walk, run, swim, and climb. They can also move in many ways that other animals cannot. They can ride bicycles, drive cars, fly airplanes, and ride skateboards to get from place to place.

Living things have senses

Senses help animals find food and avoid danger. Most people see with their eyes, hear with their ears, smell with their noses, taste with their tongues, and feel with their skin. Other living things use senses in different ways.

Some butterflies and birds can **sense** when it is time to fly to warmer places.

Grasshoppers and other insects taste with their feet and smell with their **antennae**.

(above) The star-nosed mole lives underground. To find food, it uses its feelers like fingers.

(right) Birds can see colors that other animals cannot see.

(left) Some bats have small eyes. They find their way in the dark by making sounds and listening for echoes.

Where is home?

Living things are all over the world! Plants grow in hot, cold, wet, and dry places. Animals live where plants grow. They need plants for food. Animals also use plants as their homes. They live in trees, under bushes, and among weeds.

Look at the small pictures on this page and name some plants and animals that live in each place.

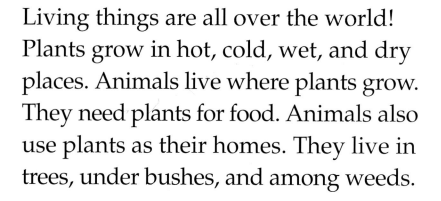

This termitary has tunnels, rooms, and thousands of termites inside.

Some animals work hard to build homes. Birds make nests. Termites build huge homes called **termitaries**. They use saliva and soil to build tall towers that are full of tunnels. The termites live in the tunnels.

People build the biggest and strongest homes. They have built houses and buildings in areas where plants and animals once lived. Sometimes people forget that other living things need places to live, too.

Making babies

All living things come from other living things. Adult living things have **offspring**. Plants make seeds, which grow into new plants. Birds lay eggs from which baby birds hatch. People have children.

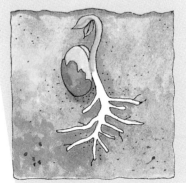

seeds

new plant

(top) Many birds such as the great egret are excellent parents.

(above) Crayfish babies hang onto their mother's legs.

(left) Mammal mothers such as horses look after their babies for a long time.

People are the same...

In some ways, people are the same as other living things. They are made of cells. They need air, water, food, and light. They grow, change, move, and make babies. Like other living things, people die.

...and different

There are many ways in which people are different from other living things. They can use their minds to learn and solve difficult problems.

People wear clothes. Some clothes are plain, and other clothes are fancy. People use languages to speak to one another. Many people speak more than one language. People can learn how to read and write. They use their imaginations to draw and paint.

Picture glossary & index

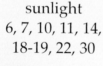

8 9 0   Printed in the U.S.A.   7 6